Grieving:
Our Path
Back to Peace

Grieving:
Our Path
Back to Peace

JAMES R.
WHITE

BETHANY HOUSE PUBLISHERS
MINNEAPOLIS, MINNESOTA 55438

Grieving: Our Path Back to Peace
Copyright © 1997
James R. White

Scripture quotations identified NASB are taken from the NEW
AMERICAN STANDARD BIBLE®, Copyright © 1960, 1962, 1963,
1968, 1971, 1972, 1973, 1975, 1977, 1995 by the Lockman
Foundation. Used by permission.

Published by Bethany House Publishers
A Ministry of Bethany Fellowship International
11400 Hampshire Avenue South
Minneapolis, Minnesota 55438
www.bethanyhouse.com

Printed in the United States of America by
Bethany Press International, Minneapolis, Minnesota 55438

Library of Congress Cataloging-in-Publication Data

White, James R. (James Robert), 1962–
    Grieving: our path back to peace / by James R. White.
      p. cm.
    ISBN 0-7642-2000-4
    1. Grief—Religious aspects—Christianity. 2. Bereavement—
Religious aspects—Christianity. I. Title.
BV4905.2.W513   1997
248.8'66—dc21   97–33828
                                                          CIP

*This book is lovingly dedicated to the memory
of Autumn Dawn Middleton.
She lived only a short while on this earth,
but in that brief time she brought joy
into the lives of so many, including, especially,
her grandpa Mike Middleton,
for whom this book is also written.*

JAMES R. WHITE is director of Alpha and Omega Ministries, a Christian apologetics organization based in Phoenix, Arizona. He teaches for Golden Gate Baptist Theological Seminary's Arizona Campus, Grand Canyon University, and Faraston Theological Seminary. He is also a critical consultant on the *New American Standard Bible* update, and has served as staff chaplain at Thunderbird Samaritan Hospital. He is the author of several books.

Contents

one

Autumn's Grandpa Mike

When I picked up the phone I thought my friend Mike was calling about my computer. He had kept me sane during the preceding weeks when I was going through "upgrade trauma," and I thought he was calling about the next item we needed to replace. I was wrong.

"Jim," he said, his voice strangely thin. "I lost my granddaughter last night. She's gone."

Ministers and those who have worked as hospital chaplains have this strange belief that they are supposed to have immediate answers in such situations. We think we are supposed to be superhuman or something and always prepared for such an announcement. I proved my humanity by responding with nothing more than, "What?"

Mike went on to tell me more about what had happened. His granddaughter, Autumn Dawn, had been born four weeks and one day earlier. I remembered his joy and pride at his first grandchild. But now she was gone, and as Mike said, "Last night I just wanted to die. I've lived forty-seven years in this world and made a mess of things. Why couldn't God take me and leave her?"

I had gathered enough of my wits about me to realize that now was not the time for in-depth theological analysis of the transcendent reasons behind this tragedy. There would be time enough for that another day. For now, I simply wanted to be there for my friend, so I asked if there was anything I could do.

The viewing was Friday night. I've done my share of funerals, having worked as a hospital chaplain, so I am not a stranger to death. But there is simply something "wrong" with seeing a twenty-nine-day-old baby girl in a funeral chapel. My mind didn't want to accept the reality before me. I held Mike and we cried together.

The funeral was the next morning. The congregation of Mike's church was there for him. His pastor did a masterful job. I don't believe I could have made it through such an experience. I simply can't control my tears well enough. They took the tiny cradle out of the church and whisked it away in a hearse. Words failed me.

That night I made up a card for Mike. I inserted some pictures I had obtained of Autumn from a memorial Mike put on the Internet for her.[1] Accompanied by my seven-year-old daughter, Summer Marie, I went over to Mike's house to deliver the card. After spending some time in the house, we went outside. As I was getting ready to leave, I gave Mike a hug. There was a moment of silence, and then Summer threw her arms open wide and said, "My turn!" As Mike knelt down to receive from Summer the greatest gift she

---

[1]http://www.periprod.com/autumn/

could give him, I thought about how wonderful it is that God puts others in our lives.

And so begins a process in Mike's life. The viewing and the funeral are just the beginning. The process of grieving has now begun. It will not be an orderly process. It will oftentimes call him into the darkest alleys of emotional pain, and at times propel him into confusion, sadness, and even, once in a while, joy. But it is a process that he will go through for two simple reasons: he is human, and he loved. Since he is human, he will grieve, for God designed us that way. And since he opened his heart and loved his granddaughter, Autumn Dawn, he will grieve the loss of that special little girl. Anyone who is old enough to love is old enough to grieve. Fight as we might against it, that is the way God made us.

Christians Grieve, Too

My friend Mike enters into grief as a Christian. There is no promise in Scripture that says a believer will be spared these kinds of tragedies—none at all. The promise is that God will be with those who mourn, not that He will keep them from such things. But what will it mean to Mike that he goes into this process believing that Jesus Christ died and rose again? How will this impact his grief?

Sadly, some Christians think that they should not grieve. "My loved one is in a better place, so why should I grieve?" Yes, your loved one may well be in a better place, but you have lost an important part of your life, and that causes mourning and grief. We miss that person and the love we shared. Being a Christian does not remove your human feelings from you. You will grieve that loss, just like every other human being.

So what is the difference? The apostle Paul summed up the difference very well when he wrote to the Thessalonians about their loved ones who had died:

> But we do not want you to be uninformed, brethren, about those who are asleep, so that you will not grieve as do the rest who have no hope. For if we believe that Jesus died and rose again, even so God will bring with Him those who have fallen asleep in Jesus.
>
> 1 THESSALONIANS 4:13–14

Some might misunderstand the import of Paul's words and understand him to be saying that Christians should not grieve. That is not his point. He says that Christians should not grieve *as do the rest who have no hope.*" It is not grief that Paul says the believer should not experience: it is grief *without hope.* That is the key difference.

Christians grieve, just like all other human beings. But the major and all-important difference is that Christians grieve *in hope.* They live in hope of the resurrection of the dead, made a surety in their experience by the resurrection of Jesus Christ from the dead. They live in hope of His redemption, His return, His glory. They grieve knowing the truth of Paul's words to the Corinthians:

> *Blessed be the God and Father of our Lord Jesus Christ, the Father of mercies and God of all comfort, who comforts us in all our affliction so that we will be able to comfort those who are in any affliction with the comfort with which we ourselves are comforted by God.*
>
> 2 CORINTHIANS 1:3–4

Available to the Christian is the comfort of God himself. The One who gave His own Son on our behalf, and who certainly knows, then, the depths of love in that self-sacrificial love of the Cross, promises to comfort us in our pain and sorrow. That is why the Christian grieves, *but in hope*.

As we briefly discuss the grieving process, we will often find that the believer and nonbeliever alike share the same experiences. But when it comes to the point of how one moves through the process and how one *views* grief, the issue of *hope* will be seen over and over again.

What is the grieving process like? How can we make sense of it? Let's find out.

two

Am I the Only One Who Feels This Way?

I have no energy. I feel as if there is a weight lying upon my chest, holding me back, making it difficult to get up in the morning or do anything all day long. I can't concentrate. Tasks that used to be easy for me are now difficult. The future looks so black and bleak. There's just too much to handle. I don't know how I can go on.

Ever since I lost my loved one, my life has been a shambles. Oh, I managed to make it through the funeral all right. Many commented on how "strong" I was. Little did *they* know what was going on inside me. But once the relatives left and the friends stopped calling, it all began to collapse in upon me. The loneliness. The feelings I never expected and still don't understand. I weep at the slightest provocation: I can't even see it coming. I find myself standing in the aisle at the grocery store crying at the sight of a favorite food that brings back such a poignant memory. I do double takes while driving, thinking for a moment that I've seen my loved one walking on the sidewalk, and then I feel so stupid for doing the same thing over and over again. I'm on an emotional roller coaster, and I don't know if I will ever be able to get off.

I can't control my emotions—any of them. I get angry so much more easily than I used to. I'm sick and tired of people telling me they understand, when I know they *don't* understand at all! How could they? I've been offended many times, and I know in my heart those people really meant no harm. I'm afraid some of my relationships may have been forever damaged by things said since the death.

If those words sound familiar to you, you are not alone. They describe just some of the common experiences of people in grief. And when you've lost a loved one, you will grieve. You will either work through the grief to your benefit, or, by some mechanism or another, you'll put off elements of it until later, and that to your detriment. But grieve you will. God made us that way.

One of the most important things I've learned in grief counseling is this: you need to realize that the feelings you are having, the troubles you are experiencing, *are not abnormal or unusual.* That is, feelings of loneliness, fear, confusion, dread of the future, and even anger are not unique to you. You are not the first person to feel these things, even if you did not *expect* to feel them when, in those quiet moments before this happened, you considered the possibility of what life would be like without that special person.

Our culture has done everything in its power to rid itself of having to think of death and its consequences. As a result, we don't talk about it, think about it, or do a very good job preparing ourselves for its certain arrival. As a result, we enter into the grieving process unprepared for what lies ahead. We don't realize the range of emotions we are going to face, and we often don't even know how to reach out to those around us for their help and comfort. What's even worse is that many feel uneasy giving comfort, because it isn't "the thing to do" in our society. We are all supposed to be able to "handle things on our own." Well, grief is not handled well alone. God made us social beings, and when we lose a loved one, we desire and need the help and assistance of others.

Give Yourself Time!

The first thing to realize about the grieving process is that you can't sit down and chart out how long it is going to take you to "get through it." In fact, in a very important sense you will *never* "get through it." That is, you will always be a bereaved person. That relationship that was yours with husband, wife, brother, sister, mother, father, son, daughter, grandparent, grandchild, or simply close friend will never be there again in this life. It is an unalterable fact that will change the course of the rest of your life. So in some senses you will always be "in the process." You may well shed a tear twenty years from now on an anniversary or birthday, *and there isn't anything wrong with that*. One does not seek to escape grief, but to embrace it, work through it, allow it to heal the hurt, so that we can move on with our lives in full light and recognition of what has happened and how God has changed our lives as a result.

But there are other ways of viewing the process as something that we do, eventually, work through and complete. And as with any process of life, *it takes time.* You simply cannot compare yourself to someone else and say, "Well, Aunt Charlene was back on her feet and seemed just fine about two months after Uncle Dave died, so I guess I should have been through with this by then, too." You were not married to Uncle Dave. You did not have the relationship that Charlene had with him and hence cannot even begin to really know what issues Charlene had to face in her grief. What is more, any grief counselor will tell you that two months is a very short period of time. Most people do not feel the full force of their loss and the emotional toll it will exact for a good four to six months after the loss. Many report that the fifth, sixth, and seventh months are the darkest and most difficult. Of course, in our society you are expected to be "over it" in about two weeks and back to work, ready to put it all behind you. Our society really doesn't handle grief very well.

In counseling with those who have suffered a loss, I have often had to point out that the greatest pressure being exerted upon them was not coming from friends, relatives, or even employers. *It was coming from themselves!* You may not be able to do anything about the employer who won't give you the time you need, but you can surely do something about yourself!

Decide, right now, to allow the natural grieving

process to take the time it needs to take. Not more time than it needs, not less time than it needs, but just what it needs to bring you to the position where you can live in full light of your loss and yet do so with the joy and fulfillment that God intends His children to have.

How long will that be for you? No one knows. One thing is for certain: it can't be shortened. Your makeup, the relationship you have lost, and the factors that went into the loss all come together to determine how long the process will last. For example, if you have lost your husband or wife of many years, the grieving process will "look" much different than if you have lost a newborn infant. Why? Well, one major reason is that you have formed habits of life with that husband or wife that, in many ways, define who you are as a person. The newborn infant's loss does not involve long-lasting habits. The pain is just as severe, but the process of grieving that loss will differ in many respects from the loss of one's husband or wife.

There are all sorts of complicating factors that enter into how long it will take for grief to take its course. The nature of the relationship you had, how close you were, whether there were unresolved issues between you, the way in which death came (suddenly, in an accident or heart attack, or over a long period of time, due to something like cancer)—all these things have their voice in determining how much work you will have to do (and it is work, mind you!) to complete the course. That is why no two people are identical in their grief, and no one can chart out what is going to happen to anyone else as they mourn their loss.

So grieving is natural, it takes time, and it is individual. Yet it follows a pattern, as well. We can't put that pattern into black-and-white terms, but the pattern is there all the same. The pattern exists because we are all creatures created in the image of God. That unity that is ours in our creatureliness gives rise to the patterns we can observe in grief. Let's take a look at some of the common characteristics that are found in the lives of those who experience a loss.

three

The Patterns of Grief

We like to have things in our lives well organized, our tasks in order, and our emotions under control. Yet grief defies such easy categorization and instead forces us to operate on general principles. Despite this, we will see that it is possible to identify certain patterns in our experience that are found with those who have already been there.

Grief is not linear. You don't start at the loss, and then proceed in a nice straight line through phases like "anger" or "sadness" until you reach the end of the line and the end of the process. That would be nice, but God didn't make us that way.

At times grief seems, especially to those who are experiencing it, as if it is a circle. A person goes through the "resentment/bitterness/bargaining" stage and thinks, "Well, there, I've gone through that, and I'm glad I won't have to go through it again." But then, lo and behold, a few weeks later they realize they are smack dab back in the middle of the same feelings they had before! Many are tempted to give up at this point, since it seems like grief is a circle that cannot be broken. And one thing is for certain—no one wants to stay in that process for the rest of their lives!

The grieving process is not a line, neither is it a circle. Instead, we might best describe it as a spiral. From one viewpoint, a spiral looks like a circle, but from another you can see that progress is being made in one direction or another. That spiral can be headed up or down. In either case, a person traveling along that spiral may visit one stage of grief more than once, but if progress is being made, one will have learned from that stage before, and if healing is taking place, one will not stay in that stage as long as before. Each time we meet those feelings, we are a little better able to handle them, a little better able to go on with our lives.

I should note at this point that not everyone experiences all of the phases of grief. Not everyone, for example, struggles with anger. These categories are based upon the general experience of those who have lost a loved one. Every situation, as we have said, is unique, and therefore exceptions are to be expected.

The spiral of grief can either lead us upward and eventually out of the process, or if we refuse to face our grief and engage in self-destructive behavior that denies the reality of what has taken place in our lives, it can lead ever downward into despair, loneliness, and bitterness. Sadly, I have met more than one person who was still in the process many, many years after a loss. They were bitter, unhappy, and unable to function in a normal way, all due to their unwillingness to face the *necessity* of working through grief. We will talk more about the danger of this kind of situation later on. For now, we might see the two spirals of grief like this:

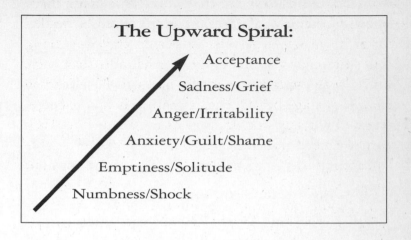

On the other hand, note the small but important differences in the opposite:

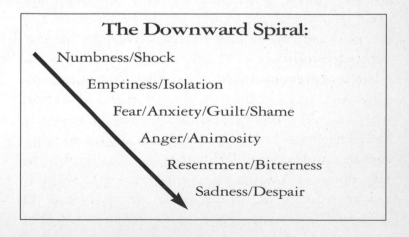

It is helpful to contrast the stages of the process between the upward and downward spirals:

The Upward Spiral	The Downward Spiral
Numbness/Shock	Numbness/Shock
Emptiness/Solitude	Emptiness/Isolation
Anxiety/Guilt/Shame	Fear/Anxiety/Guilt/Shame
Anger/Irritability	Anger/Animosity
Sadness/Grief	Resentment/Bitterness
Acceptance	Sadness/Despair

Note how these stages, which are based upon the common experience of people as they deal with their loss, are *similar* but very *different*.

Shock

Everyone goes through numbness and shock: it is in reality God's gracious way of helping us to cope with those first few days and weeks after the loss itself. Our minds are not allowed to process fully what has happened. We handle things in an almost mechanical way. Many are tempted to think that we are being so strong, so courageous, when the simple fact of the matter is we are on "auto-pilot," going about the many tasks we have to accomplish without really being aware of everything that is happening around us. Some are concerned about the accompanying numbness, the lack of emotion that some exhibit. But during the first two weeks or so after a loss, such a lack of feeling is probably much more related to emotional shock than anything else. Sadly, our society often gives us only a few weeks to "adjust," so that just as the shock is wearing off and the full force of the loss is hitting us, we are expected to put this all aside and "get back to business."

Solitude Versus Isolation

Next we have, in the upward spiral, emptiness and solitude (the order of presentation is not meant to indicate a particular order that these stages will follow). Everyone feels a tremendous sense of emptiness and separation, and for good reason: a large portion of their world has just disappeared, and we very much want things to be what they once were. But those on the upward spiral experience solitude, while those on the downward spiral experience isolation. What is the difference?

Solitude is necessary at times during the grieving process. We need time to ourselves to think, reflect, and mourn. This is fine and proper. But there is a difference between solitude and isolation. With solitude, you have periods of quiet interspersed with normal interaction with loved ones and friends. Isolation speaks of a person pushing others away, making an active choice to sever relationships and refuse consolation and comfort. People who isolate themselves cut themselves off from positive, healthy input from outside their world of hurt, and they do so to their own detriment. As much as we might want the world to "go away," we still live in the world and cannot isolate ourselves from others. Cutting yourself off from family, fellow believers, and friends is the first step toward embarking on the downward spiral of grief rather than the upward track.

Anxiety

Next we have anxiety, guilt, and shame. Most people who grieve feel anxious for many reasons. We are always reminded of our own mortality when someone close to us dies. Christians should experience this less than nonbelievers for the simple reason that we should always be reminded of the death of our Lord. We should have a very realistic view of death, including our own, and should live each day in light of the fact that we are but a mere breath that, someday, will pass from this earth (Psalm 39:5). But no matter how often we think of it, the passing of a loved one reminds us that we, too, are destined for death.

Anxiety also comes if we were dependent in any way upon the person who has gone. Wives who lose husbands are often anxious about many things: how they will live, how they will care for the house and take care of things the husband always did, etc. Parents who lose one child become anxious about the welfare of other children. Children who lose one parent become anxious for the other who is still living. Another term used today for *anxiety* is *stress*, and we all know how much of that we live with every day. Believers have the promise of God that we can cast our cares (our anxieties, our "stress," if you will) upon Him, for He cares for us (1 Peter 5:6–7). Such is a precious promise for the Christian who is grieving.

Guilt is a tough issue to deal with. Yet I have seen it tear apart many a person who was struggling with grief. "If I had only seen the signs earlier," the wife says after her husband dies of a heart attack. "If I had only driven that night," the husband says after his wife dies in a car accident. "Second-guessing" is another way of describing this common activity. We are always looking to lay blame somewhere, and often, even if we don't do it openly, we lay it upon ourselves.

Again, the Christian has the wonderful comfort of knowing that all his or her guilt, including guilt that comes to us in grief, is carried to the Cross in our Savior. We know that second-guessing God will accomplish nothing (though we can't avoid the questions that come to our minds), and even if the grieving process is very difficult, believers who go through it come out with a firmer trust in the sovereignty and goodness of God. We will discuss the "tough questions" about God's goodness later.

One might wonder how shame fits into this.

Sometimes it comes in the form of shame for not having done more, even when there wasn't anything more we could have done. This is pretty much the same as second-guessing. Parents who lose children often feel ashamed of themselves *as parents*, thinking that if they had just "been there" they could have prevented the death. But others speak of shame in the sense that they now feel outcast. Their identity was so much defined by the other person (this is especially true of widows) that they now feel like an unknown person. Their friends are uncomfortable around them because of the loss, and now they feel ashamed.

But the difference between the upward spiral and the downward one is seen in the addition of fear to the downward side. A person who is becoming isolated is likely to fear many things. Fear feeds on isolation, and isolation feeds on fear. When we are separated from those around us, we begin to fear everyone and everything. Every person I have ever counseled who had become trapped in the cycle experienced fear, especially of the future. Widows are especially subject to this kind of problem. For them the future is a dark morass, and many have no desire whatsoever to press on with life.

The believer again has the promise of God that He holds the future in His hand, that He has a purpose in each one's life, and that He will never leave nor forsake them. The strong light of His love can pierce the blackest darkness we see ahead of us, and His hand can guide us through the difficulties of life, even death itself. The Christian is not given a spirit of fear, but of power, love, and discipline (2 Timothy 1:7). The Spirit who dwells within us raised Jesus Christ from the dead, and He can surely bear us up through our trials and difficulties. As Paul reminded us, "For you have not received a spirit of slavery leading to fear again, but you have received a spirit of adoption as sons by which we cry out, 'Abba! Father!' " (Romans 8:15).

Anger

Anger is arguably the strongest human emotion. It is certainly the most dangerous in the grieving process. Almost everyone experiences anger when faced with the loss of a loved one. That anger is often expressed toward others, sometimes with reason, sometimes without. Anger would be naturally expressed against the drunk driver who kills a child or spouse. But how do we deal with anger when cancer is the culprit? How can one be "angry" with cancer? We often express that anger toward family and friends, resulting in many a ruptured relationship. We might turn the anger in upon ourselves, berating ourselves for some unspoken word, some unresolved conflict. And we all must admit that at times we are angry with God. Yes, even believers can feel anger toward God for their loss, and anyone who denies this is possible simply isn't being honest. Thankfully, God is big enough to handle our anger and our tough questions.

We should also mention the fact that, surprising as it is to many, there are folks who feel anger *toward the person who has died.* I have seen people in a grief counseling group gasp when I mentioned this, and say something like, "I didn't think anyone else ever felt like this! I've been so ashamed for being angry at my husband for leaving me, when I know such thinking is irrational and foolish!" At times we feel angry because our loved one didn't take care of himself or herself, and hence hastened death. Or that person "was always doing dangerous things." Often a widow will feel anger at being left alone, unable to do some of the most basic things in life. She may feel anger that he didn't "prepare" things better, or that her lifelong dreams of what old age was going to be like have been shattered by his death. We hate to admit it, but we get angry when our dreams are taken away from us, and we will express that anger in one way or another.

Anger must be dealt with. It cannot be ignored. Anger is a very strong emotion and, if left to itself, will trap us in destructive attitudes and viewpoints. The Christian has a means of dealing with anger, for the opposite of anger is love, and the resources of love available to the person redeemed in Christ is inexhaustible. The salve for anger is forgiveness, and since the believer has been forgiven in Christ, he or she can likewise forgive. We will talk more about this later.

Anger will also express itself in irritability. Grieving makes us emotionally vulnerable on many fronts, and this is certainly one of them. We take offense at the slightest statement. I can't count how many people have spoken to me about what "Joel said to Cathy at the viewing," or how "Bob treated Mary's family so shabbily" after the funeral. We need to realize that everyone who is impacted by the death is in emotional turmoil and is therefore likely to take offense at things that otherwise would be overlooked. Sometimes we say things we don't mean to say or express thoughts that we otherwise would keep to ourselves. All of this adds up to a very explosive situation, and many a family can testify to the aftermath. While it would be nice if everyone went into the situation with the realization that they are going to need to be very patient, very few grieving people are concerned about working on their patience at that moment. One negative side of grief is that it focuses us inward upon ourselves, often leading to lapses of patience and gentleness with those around us.

The downward spiral of grief replaces irritability, which is a passing thing, with animosity, which is described as ill will or resentment tending toward hostile action. It speaks to an attitude over time. Animosity is the natural result of isolation and fear. A frightened animal will lash out at any perceived danger. A person who has become isolated and who is experiencing fear will often react in animosity toward others. Anger, the battery acid of emotions, begins to eat away at the very fabric of the person's soul, and surely such a situation expresses itself toward those who are outside the ever shrinking and dark world of such a person's mind. That is why anger *must* be dealt with and cannot be ignored. Left to itself, it causes great damage.

Sadness

The upward spiral of grief separates from the downward version in moving to those times of sadness and mourning that most people associate with the loss of a loved one. Sometimes the sadness can be particularly intense and debilitative. Birthdays, anniversaries, and holidays will often bring on intense sadness and grief. But sometimes we simply don't know why we find ourselves sitting around and crying, unable— or unwilling—to do anything at all.

Sadness can also be "chronic," in the sense of that feeling deep down in the chest that won't go away. It doesn't keep us from getting things done, but it certainly saps our strength and joy. It's not the first thing on our mind, but it's always there in the background, just beyond our touch. We find ourselves thinking about it when we should be doing something else, or it will intrude itself into our thoughts at inopportune times. It makes solemn moods deeper and pulls happy times down just a bit. We know it is there, but we can't seem to do anything about it.

If you are in the midst of grief right now, you may

not believe what I am about to say, but it is true none-theless. Over time, if you are facing your sadness and dealing with those issues that must be handled, these periods of sadness and that dull ache in your chest will diminish in intensity and duration, and eventually they will go away. Yes, as I said before, you may well shed a tear and feel that old sadness many years down the road, but there is hope at the end of the tunnel. While the process does not go as fast as popular opinion would have us to believe, it does reach a point of resolution, eventually.

Resentment/Bitterness

The downward spiral of grief includes one phase that is not found in the upward version in any form: resentment and bitterness. It is easy to see why: if we have avoided isolation, fear, and animosity, we will not be led into resentment and bitterness. But the next logical step in that chain is a hardened attitude that can bring nothing but deep and abiding sadness and despair (the final phase on this downward spiral). Since issues have been left unresolved, since friends have been kept at arm's length, and since anger has been eating away at the heart, a set attitude of re-sentment of others and their happiness, and bitterness toward the world at large can set in. I have, sadly, met more than one person who in their old age is resentful and bitter toward anyone and everyone, and upon do-ing some digging, I discovered that such a person had experienced a deep loss earlier in life, and they had never allowed grief to do what God intends it to do. As a result, they have become hardened, difficult, unloving individuals. It is not a pretty picture.

The Key to the Patterns of Grief

The end of the downward spiral is despair. What is the opposite of despair? It is a four letter word— *hope.* The key, I truly believe, for any person who wishes to work through grief and experience once again the fullness of life and its joys is hope. For the Christian, it is the one thing that separates him or her from those who do not know Christ.

Hope is the key to the grieving process. It is what makes the difference between being in the downward spiral, headed to despair, and the upward spiral, leading to acceptance of one's loss and the ability to once again love and rejoice and feel with all of one's heart. Hope will determine which direction a person will travel and how fully a person will experience the healing power of the grieving process. This was Paul's point in writing to the Thessalonians, for he well knew the role of hope in the Christian life. It is the power that keeps one going, the fuel that runs the engine of the soul, the medicine that brings healing to a wounded heart. It gives strength to face an uncertain future, for it looks not to its own resources, but to Christ.

When we have hope we do not isolate ourselves from family, friends, or God's people. When we have hope for the future we do not live in fear, but in anticipation of God's continuing work in our lives. When we have hope we do not develop a hard edge of anger toward others. It is what rescues us from the pitfalls and dangers of grief. It makes grief a means of healing rather than a snare that holds us in perpetual sadness.

At times even a Christian will despair of hope. It may be during those long dark nights when our heart aches the most that our hope seems to have vanished. But hope and faith are the works of the Spirit in a person's heart, and God will be faithful to those who are His. While the flame of hope may grow dim and seem to have gone out, it will flare up yet again in the hearts of those who have by grace known Christ.

It's Not Too Late

Are you on the downward spiral? It's not too late. Yes, the grieving process has been elongated, so to speak, for you. But that is in the past. The issue now is to press forward in the right direction. What can you do?

First, have you cut yourself off from the very sources God intended to assist you? Are you isolated from others? If so, why? Can you reach out to the support system of friends, family, and church? If you are isolated by geographical location, can you find other ways to have fellowship with others? And most important, have you isolated yourself from God, as well? When we have no one else in this world we always have God, and He will bear you up, if you will let Him.

Have you sought to artificially shorten your grief by refusing to deal with important aspects of the process? Ask God to strengthen you to deal with those things that you know you have avoided.

Above all, simply recognizing your condition is the most important step in reversing your direction and getting on the right track. Such an admission on your part indicates an honesty that will help you to deal with fear, animosity, and despair. Those who have started downward on the spiral *can* reverse direction. Hope is the key. Hope accepts the promises of God and trusts in Him. That is the means of your deliverance.

four

The Work of Grieving

While grief is certainly disorderly, and while you may revisit various stages and emotions more than once during your grieving, there is a way of looking at the process that might be helpful. In a very general, overarching way, we could divide the process up into four phases:

Shock and numbness
Working through feelings
Unlearning old patterns and learning new ones
Reentry

This oversimplified view doesn't deal with the specific feelings one experiences, but rather with what grief *should be doing* in a person's life. And I cannot stress enough the fact that the two middle items involve *work*. Grieving is *work*, no matter how else we may look at it. The person who decides to be diligent in doing that work will find the experience no less painful, but will certainly find it to pass more quickly.

The outline above is especially helpful in aiding us in getting the "broad picture." Shock and numbness come first. Then we are faced with the storm of feelings and emotions, and we must work through them, face them, and learn from them. Then comes the time when we must engage in the long and tedious work of unlearning old habits, habits tied to the person who has gone from us, and learning new ones that are based upon our new reality in life. This, too, takes time and effort, but eventually allows us to move to the point of reentry into "normal" emotional life, a life marked by joys and sorrows, but not marked by the constant remembrance of the loved one who has died.

Working Through the Emotions

The primary job we face when dealing with our emotions is simply being honest with ourselves. Many people are concerned about the *depth* and *range* of emotions they encounter in grief, and end up burying various feelings out of fear or shame. Yet we must be honest with the feelings we are experiencing. That doesn't mean we have to go around telling everyone else what we are experiencing in every instance, but surely we must be honest with ourselves and with those who are closest to us, including the Lord through prayer. Of course, God is well aware of what we are feeling, so trying to deceive Him is impossible anyway. And here is another gift of grace for the Christian, for the Lord, who knows our hearts, is always with us and accepts us even in our pain and confusion.

At the beginning, we should simply seek to take it one day at a time, knowing that we simply cannot be prepared for what lies ahead of us. Many people, especially those who have watched a loved one die over a long period of time due to cancer or some similar disease, think they are "ready" for that death, but I have found that as long as life exists, we cannot enter fully into the grieving process. Oh yes, such a person may indeed experience *elements* of the process even before death, due to the debilitation of their loved one, but no one can be prepared for the full process until life itself has ended.

Dealing With the Good Cry

Sometimes you will just "sense" a good cry coming on. You eventually give up trying to figure out what triggered it—most of the time you can't figure it out anyway (grief is not a logical thing). But you know it is headed your direction. What do you do? Well, fighting it probably won't work, and if you do fight it and lose, you'll just feel twice as bad. So I suggest that if you feel a real good cry coming on, it's time to make something positive out of it. Go get that photo album you've been hiding in the closet, and if you are going to cry, you might as well make it a positive experience mixed with joy at the memories brought back by those pictures.

As I've mentioned before, our society doesn't handle grief well and will often tell people that crying is somehow "bad" for them. Of course, if it is a daily or hourly experience, that would be true. But our society has gone to the other extreme in removing our natural and healthy expressions of sadness from us and re-

placing them with something like, "Hey, be a man."
While there is a place for a positive exhortation to
move on with life, take courage in the Lord, and experience His joy in service to others, there is also the
recognition of the importance of tears. There is nothing wrong with weeping. Even the Lord Jesus, when
faced with the tragedy of death and decay, wept (John
11:35). You will shed many a tear when working
through the emotions that come on the heels of death.
It is okay to cry, and I say that to *both* men and women.

Men are often ashamed by the emotions they feel
when grieving, but there is no reason for shame. God
made us feeling beings, and we dare not shortchange
ourselves simply because our society has a very un-
realistic view of what it means to be a "man."

Transitions

As we work through our feelings and accept their
healing role in our suffering (i.e., as we move upward
on the spiral of grief), we begin to see, if dimly at first,
that we are in a period of transition. We are changing
because our life has changed. Our situation has been
altered drastically, and we must adjust to the new reality. Many find this to be one of their greatest sources
of anger, by the way. "I liked my life the way it was,
and I am angry, *very angry*, that my life has been
changed." Yet changed it has, and the sooner we are
able to grasp this reality and *embrace it through God's*

grace, the sooner we will make it through the grieving process.

The severity of the transition through which one goes after a loss is in direct proportion to how central to our life the person was who has been taken from us. If our father or mother has gone, were we particularly close to him or her so that he or she was a part of our daily life? If so, the transition will be great. Had our wife or husband become *the* source of our self-identification? Then again, when he or she is gone, such a transition is going to be major, and the process long. Did we lose a friend with whom we shared everything? Expect a significant transition.

Obviously, the loss of a distant relative or a neighbor with whom we had little contact does not impact us the way the loss of someone very close to us does. The more vital a part of our life that person was, the more deeply we will feel the loss, and the longer it will take to transition from what "was" to what "is."

One might see this period of transition as a relationship changing from one of flesh-and-blood contact to one of memories. One day we were speaking with and touching our loved one. The next day we can no longer do this. The shock of bereavement is just a symptom of the fact that we cannot immediately process the reality that our lives have been so drastically changed. But over time we begin to experience that relationship in a different way: through memories. At first this hurts, and many experience times in their lives when they want to do anything *but* remember! But as time heals the wounds we begin to dwell upon the good memories, and our relationship becomes one of thought rather than of direct contact. Eventually we can talk of our loved one who has gone without breaking down, and can recall memories, both good and bad, without undue pain or remorse. This is the natural progression of events.

Much of the upheaval in our lives that is prevalent during the grieving process comes from the fact that we are "in between." We are in the process of unlearning old habits and learning new ones. Just as there is a stage in the cleaning of a room where things look a whole lot worse than they did when you started, so, too, the transition period is marked by unfinished projects and misplaced parts of our lives.

A common example of how we are creatures of habit who must learn, over time, new habits has to do with the "mistaken phone call." A person who has lost someone will be at work and will experience something good, or will hear some particular important piece of news. The first impulse is to grab the phone and dial that number. Somewhere along the line the hand stops and the heart pounds as the realization comes crashing home: "I can't call him because he isn't here anymore." What may have started as a joyous thing ends up becoming a negative because of the simple mistake, borne out of habit. If this has happened to you, take heart. It happens to us all.

We naturally think of telling our loved ones about what is happening in our lives. When they go, it takes time for us to get used to the new set of realities that marks our life. We will make mistakes—sometimes painful mistakes—but eventually we will learn the new habits and will pick up the phone and call that other person who has, in some sense, taken that important role in our life.

The Matter of Belongings

One of the toughest items we deal with has to do with the belongings of our loved one. Widows have been known to simply close "that" closet and leave it alone for years simply because they could not bring themselves to look at the clothes and other personal items that remind them so strongly of "him." Even the smell of his personal items, that faint yet unmistakable scent of his favorite after-shave, is too much to be handled, especially alone.

In the same way, the parents who have lost a child may dread the process of going into the child's room and dealing with the toys, the pictures, the little clothes. At times it seems almost easier to just close the room off and forget it than it is to face that pile of painful reminders.

Belongings can be a source of real difficulty, not only for the person who does not want to face them, but also in the family where problems erupt over "who gets what." While it is easier to say than to deal with, things are just things, and it is better to maintain relationships over time than it is to have a particular possession. Those who are in grief over a loss frequently have trouble looking outside themselves at the "bigger picture," but by God's grace we can save ourselves a lot of heartache if we put some effort into keeping peace in the family at a difficult time.

There are two extremes to be avoided when it comes to the disposition of belongings. First, don't go for the "get rid of it all" option. Some people, unable to face the task of sorting through the belongings of the loved one, have asked others to come in and basically "take it all away." Then, later, after the first intense feelings of loss have subsided, such a person begins wishing for a particular item, a picture, or a book, but it is too late. Everything is already gone. This is a most unfortunate circumstance.

On the other hand, it would be a severe mistake to create a "shrine." This happens when a person sets up a special room with certain belongings of the loved one, never to be touched. Such a shrine becomes an ever-present reminder of the loss rather than a positive way of remembering certain aspects of that person's life. A person who is tempted to make shrines may be having trouble accepting the reality of the loss itself, and may be doing things to avoid facing the truth.

If you can't handle the task of dealing with possessions by yourself, ask a close friend or relative to go with you into that room, that closet, that storage shed. It may not be a wonderfully positive experience, but sharing it with someone else can make the burden a good bit lighter. Keep those things you really want, and give away what you don't want. If you are uncertain, keep them around for a while. If later on, when you have a more balanced viewpoint, you wish to give them away, you can. But if you give it all away and later want something, you might not be able to get it back. Be conservative, but most important, deal with the task before you. The longer you put it off, the bigger it will grow in your mind. Once you've tackled it, you will feel better.

We've now talked some about the *work* involved in grieving. There are also some dangers, some pitfalls, to be avoided, as well. To these we now turn.

five

Avoiding the Pitfalls

Like any human process, grieving has its dangers, its pitfalls. There are little trapdoors here, little detours there, that can make us waste precious time and energy. A little forewarning can help us to keep on the straight and narrow and arrive at our destination in the best possible time.

Some of the topics addressed below are theological, some deal with our emotions, and some are downright practical. But they all speak to realities experienced by grieving people every day.

You Can't Go Back

One of the most insidious and dangerous aspects of grief can be summed up in one quotation: "I just want to get back to the way I was." Now, that line may not strike you as particularly wrong at the first reading, but I have found the attitude it expresses to be one of the most difficult things to address in grief counseling. I have met people whose grief was being prolonged unnecessarily because they could not see the trap that lies behind those words.

You see, six months from now you will be a different person than you are today. You will grow, learn, and change—maybe not a lot, but the difference will be there. You see, none of us can "get back to" where we were "before." Time marches on, as they say, and while we often joke about the fact that we are all aging, the fact is that we are also all *changing*. It is the inevitable result of living life.

A person who loses a loved one may begin to look back upon life "before" and start to see it in the most glowing colors. "Things were so good back then," they are tempted to think. "If I can just make things like they were back then." Many times I've discovered that in reality things were *not* all that good back then, but that isn't the issue anymore. The desire to restore things to "normal" and to "be the person I once was" becomes the driving factor in the thinking of the bereaved person.

You need to spend some time thinking about a simple fact: you can't get back to where you were. Even if you could have your loved one back, you would still be a different person than you once were. Of course, you can't have your loved one back, so getting "back" is not possible. You are a changed person. Your world has changed. That is the reality before you, and as a believer, it is a reality that has come into your life through the wise, though often inscrutable, providence of God. He will give you the grace to handle your new situation, but you need to face the fact that this new situation exists. If you continue to seek to get "back," you will unnecessarily prolong the grieving process. Eventually you will realize the truth that you and your world have been changed—grief has a way of proving this to us—but it is far better to make that decision on your own so that you can move ahead.

Many struggle with accepting their new reality and the changed person they have become because of their loss. If we did not believe that God is in control and that all things work to our good (Romans 8:28), we might well have a real problem here. But again the believer has the security in grief that comes from knowing God and His promises. We know that in all things God is working to conform us to the image of Christ, and we can be confident, even when we can't see the *how*, that in our pain and sorrow we are being made more like Christ, who himself was known as the Man of Sorrows (Isaiah 53:3).

It's Okay to Be Happy

It's been four months since the loss. You've managed to drag yourself out of the house and have joined some friends for an evening of bowling. You let one fly and manage to get just the right spin on the ball! A strike! You whirl around and let out a yell, hands in the air. You're the best! And then, like a lightning bolt out of the blue, you find yourself feeling . . . guilty! Yes, guilty for enjoying life, guilty for being happy, even though your loved one is not there to enjoy it with you.

Others in grief feel the same things but may have the added idea that if they continue on with their life and enjoy the world around them, they are somehow showing "disrespect" for the person who has died. It is almost as if their sadness is seen as a memorial to the lost loved one.

If you've experienced such feelings, you are not alone. You may be saying, "How can I ever be happy again when I feel like this?" Like so much in grief, this feeling is anything but logical. In our heads we know that the loved one we have lost would be the first one to desire our happiness. They would not want us to be afraid to experience joy. But the head is eighteen inches from the heart, and what our minds know does not always translate into how our emotions respond.

Joy is a normal human emotion. It is also a part of God's will for our lives. While you may think right now that you will never experience real joy again, that simply is not the case. It is not God's will that His people live in utter despondency throughout their lives. Joy is the heritage of the godly, and as time passes and as you transition into the acceptance of who you are in the full light of your loss, you will be able to experience joy with more frequency, and most important, without guilt. There will come a day when you will settle in your mind the reality that it's okay to be happy. Remember Psalm 30:5, "For His anger is but for a moment, His favor is for a lifetime; weeping may last for the night, but a shout of joy comes in the morning."

Our Society and Death

I have commented a number of times already on how poorly our society handles the topic of death. That unwillingness to be honest with this part of human existence can present problems to the person who is undergoing the process of grief.

Americans are, by and large, afraid of talking about death. While we show it on our televisions and movie screens with frightening regularity, we almost never really *deal with it.* People die all the time in movies, but how often is the pain and resultant heartache portrayed? When the movie *Sleepless in Seattle* came out (a movie that accurately portrays many of the emotions and feelings that accompany the death of one's spouse), people were touched from coast to coast, only proving how *unusual* such an honest treatment of this subject really is.

So deep is our aversion to honest dialogue about death that we have come up with dozens of ways of saying "death" without *really* saying death. We cover over the reality with euphemisms and do everything in our power to move on to another subject as quickly as possible.

Some in our culture are even trying to do away with the funeral for the simple reason that it forces us to face mortality with a bit too much honesty. Many are the folks who do not think that children should be exposed to death and funerals, a viewpoint with which I take tremendous issue. It was not long ago that most funerals took place right within the family home, with generations in attendance. People understood that death was a reality that we would all face, and we were a much better culture for it, too. Your priorities tend to be impacted by such things, and that in a very positive direction.

A society filled with wise men and women would be a society that would understand these words from the Scriptures: "It is better to go to a house of mourning than to go to a house of feasting, because that is the end of every man, and the living takes it to heart" (Ecclesiastes 7:2). As it is, we run the other direction and prefer never to spend a moment in the house of mourning, though by so doing, we would be reminded (to our eternal benefit) that we are all mortal, and that what is important in this life is what we do for God and how we love each other. The crass materialism of our land would suffer greatly if we were to think this way, but we would be a stronger people for it.

Sadly, because we do not talk about death and are not willing to think about its results, many in our culture are uncomfortable in the presence of a person who is in sorrow. "I don't know what to say" is often what we hear. The result of this is that many a grieving person feels shut out, abandoned, and alone. Even if the bereaved person is not actually seeking to be isolated, he can be isolated by others. Even close friends can seem "distant" simply because they, like most others in our culture, are facing an "unknown" thing. This is particularly true if they have not yet lost someone very close to them. Those who have gone through the process are often the ones who are most helpful to us. In fact, this is exactly what Paul meant when he spoke of our comforting others with the comfort we ourselves have received from God (2 Corinthians 1:4).

Feelings of abandonment and rejection only add to the depth of sadness we experience while grieving. If you, by God's grace, have a friend or relative who has the wisdom and experience to walk alongside you as you grieve, not to talk your ear off, but simply to be there, you should count yourself as tremendously blessed.

The Problem of Holidays

Another major pitfall that often "sneaks up" on people is the matter of holidays. It was a regular aspect of the grief support group I headed up for a number of years: the numbers would be two to three times larger during and right after the holidays than they were in the early fall. Why? Because holidays are often one of the hardest times for the person in grief.

More than once I heard stories that ran along the same line. The family gathers for Thanksgiving, for example. Mom roasts the turkey, as she has always done. Everyone gathers at the table, the meal is set out, and then, as if everyone had been sleepwalking up to this point, the terrible realization sets in: Dad isn't here to carve the turkey. In fact, someone, out of habit, set Dad's place at the table, and no one is even willing to sit there, let alone pick up the knife and start cutting. Someone starts weeping. A child runs from the table. The day is ruined, and no one will ever forget what happened.

Holidays are filled with pitfalls and traps like these. No other time has so many traditions, so many memories. Did the person who has died trim the tree at Christmas? Did they have a special New Year's tradition? What will we do this year? How will we handle it?

Indeed, any family gathering after a loss can struggle with such difficult issues. Many families deal with the issue of whether or not they will talk about him or her. People walk around on eggshells, trying (in vain, normally) to avoid "messing up" and mentioning that person. Tensions can run high, and many wear their emotions on their sleeves.

Holidays are not alone in packing hidden dangers: birthdays, anniversaries, and any special day associated with the loved one who has died are potential emotional "bombs" waiting to go off.

All of these difficult situations can be handled through the use of one word: *communication*. We must talk with our families about these things. We dare not run headlong into the holidays, for example, without first investing some energy in planning and preparation. Who is going to do the things that Dad or Mom used to do? Which of our family traditions are we going to change, which are we going to put on a temporary "hold" (say for a couple of years), and which are we going to continue? Simply taking the time to pick up the phone and call the principle parties who will be involved in such gatherings can save you and your family a *lot* of needless heartache, I assure you.

As much as we might wish it otherwise, holidays, birthdays, anniversaries, and family gatherings are inevitably going to come to us. We can't take away all the pain these days will bring. The first Christmas will be rough, no matter how much preparation you put forth. You will notice that empty chair, that missing person, and the whole day will be marked as "our first Christmas without . . ." If you have lost the love of your life, your spouse, that first anniversary will be a dark day, no two ways about it. But still the calendar will bring that day around, and even if you plan for it, prepare for it, it will still hurt, it will still bring sorrow and tears. Till the end of your life that day will be poignant. God made us that way. If you go into these situations aware of what is coming your direction, you can at least be prepared. The pain won't go away, but you can have your support system ready to handle the strain.

Turning Inward

Finally, one special pitfall for the believer who is grieving has to do with the matter of selfishness. Grief turns us inward upon ourselves and our own pain, and rightly so, to a point. It is our world that has been torn apart, and we do need time to ourselves to put things back together again. But as with all other emotions, we tend to go overboard. The inward bent of grief can result in simple selfishness and a focus upon self rather than upon Christ and His purposes in our life.

But even here the Christian has the advantage of never being alone in grief. If we share our sorrows in prayer with Christ, we have an ever-present means of combating selfishness and the problems that come with it. As we cast our burdens upon Him, we are forced to look away from ourselves and our own pain. We are made to look up and out rather than down and in. And by this means the Lord can keep us from becoming self-centered in our attitudes and actions.

Having looked at just a few of the pitfalls inherent in the grieving process, we need to look now at some of the tough questions that we face as believers when dealing with death and its results.

six

The Tough Questions

Questions about life and death and meaning and purpose have been discussed and talked about from the beginning of time, and I can assure you, I have nothing new to add. I've read Job and the Psalms and Romans 8 and Ephesians 1 and I don't have anything to add to those passages. I can only speak as one who has sat next to the bereaved at the time of death and have, therefore, had to think carefully about the "great issues of life" on a very practical level.

The Real Issue

The toughest answers are the shortest ones, I've discovered. I find it easier to write a three hundred-page book than a ten-page paper on the same subject. Succinctness requires accuracy and penetrating analysis, and that's often much harder than the easy road of verbosity. So I'm going to pass over many of the side issues and get to the main question right away: "Why?"

When I first entered into the hospital chaplaincy, I had to honestly admit that I didn't know how I was going to handle that question the first time I faced it. "Why?" is a big question packed in a short word. And for the chaplain, it normally means, "Why, God?"

As I read books and pondered the topic, I was often faced with the "God didn't have anything to do with it" viewpoint. This perspective seeks to distance God as much as possible from the death itself, seeking only to promise that God will do His best to help the person make it through the crisis. This answer to the tough question of "why" is *very* appealing. I felt the tug to use it many times in crisis situations. And yet, I didn't.

I rarely miss a night's sleep, but one night I stayed up struggling with how to deal with that first crisis situation in the emergency room or the cardiac unit. As a Christian theologian, I was committed to the biblical view of a sovereign and omnipotent God, unchanging and unchangeable, just and loving, merciful and holy. One thing I was certain of: I couldn't change God's character in order to make my job easier.

But I also realized that more than one person with whom I would be dealing (the hospital at which I worked was not a specifically "Christian" hospital) would not approach their loss with a full or even semibiblical view of God. How then would I deal with their question, loaded as it would be with all sorts of unbiblical baggage?

As I worked through the issue in my mind, I came to a conclusion. It is not my purpose here to defend my conclusion in biblical debate, though I could certainly do that. I simply speak from my heart, trusting that my fellow believers will hear my words.

If I told someone that God had nothing to do with the death of their loved one, I might, for a moment, provide a modicum of comfort, and might, in a sense, "let God off the hook." But I came to the stark realization that if I said such a thing, I would be, in fact, cheating that person. How so? Quite simply, if I say that God has nothing to do with our deaths, *how can I honestly and consistently say that He has anything to do with our lives, either?* As I visited suffering people all through the hospital, I was sharing with them God's closeness, God's comfort, and all of this is based upon the clear biblical teaching that God has a purpose in all things, including their suffering. So deeply ingrained in me was this concept that my favorite Bible verse speaks to this topic. It is Colossians 3:3, but first, the passage in its fuller context:

> *Therefore if you have been raised up with Christ, keep seeking the things above, where Christ is, seated at the right hand of God. Set your mind on the things above, not on the things that are on earth. For you have died and your life is hidden with Christ in God. When Christ, who is our life, is revealed, then you also will be revealed with Him in glory.*
> COLOSSIANS 3:1–4

The Bible teaches that the believer has died with Christ, and his life is now hidden with Christ in God. I have often illustrated this truth using my class ring. I take the ring off, place it in the palm of my left hand, close my hand, and then cover my left hand with my right. The ring is now safely hidden away inside both of my hands. No one can touch that ring without first going through *both* of my hands. So it is with the Christian's life. My life has been hidden with Christ (the left hand) in God the Father (the right hand). Nothing can touch my life that has not been *allowed* to touch my life by passing through both the Son and the Father. Nothing, then, is going to happen to me by accident, nothing that is outside of my loving Father's control. He who spoke the worlds into existence exercises the same power in keeping me safe in His love.

Because of this great truth, I firmly believe that everything in my life—including the greatest tragedies and trials—has a purpose. I may not know what that purpose is, and often I do not. I may not find out even in this life what the purpose for a trial or difficulty was, but I don't need to know. I have God's promise, and that is good enough for me. He has promised, many times, that he is about making me like Christ, and since that is my heart's desire, I know He will be faithful in accomplishing His task.

So, if I am convinced that God is very much involved in what is happening in *life*, how can I possibly seek to avoid the obvious reality that God is just as much involved in *death*? If God can say, "Precious in the sight of the LORD is the death of His

godly ones" (Psalm 116:15), how can I say otherwise? The Psalmist said, "My times are in Your
hand" (Psalm 31:15), and I can rejoice in that, for
where else would I like my times to be? In this uncertain and changing world, it is a blessing to know
that my times are in the hand of the one whose hands
were pierced by the nails of Calvary.

And so that evening I made the decision that I
could not take the "easy road" and remove God from
the crisis. Instead, I had to take the harder road, the
road that says, "God has a purpose in this event. We
don't know what it is, and in fact, we may never
know. But we must leave that in God's hand and
trust in His promises all the same." While that
might not "preach" as well, one thing was for certain: I could then go on and speak of the fact that
God has a purpose in the life of the surviving individuals without contradicting myself. I could honestly say that God would be with them in their sorrow and would bear them up, thus accomplishing
His purpose in their lives as well. If I said in one
breath that God had been somewhere else when the
death took place, how could I in the next breath af-
firm His constancy and presence in their life now?
The price was too high: I had to remain faithful to
God's revelation of himself in Scripture, and in the
process He allowed me to give to those who would
hear the greatest promise of all: "I will never desert
you, nor will I ever forsake you" (Hebrews 13:5).

But I'm Angry. I'm Angry With God

In our moments of honest reflection, we may have to confess that in reality we are angry with God. If He is in control (and He is), then the change in my life came from His hand. And I don't like this change. I'm angry, and yes, I'm angry with God.

God is big enough to handle your anger and your probing questions. That doesn't mean He is necessarily going to provide the answers you would like or might even demand. But He understands that we struggle with His greater wisdom and His providence.

The nonbeliever is angry with God for all the wrong reasons. In fact, the Bible says that the nonbeliever is in active rebellion against God and describes the relationship between them as one marked by hostility (Romans 8:7).

But the believer's relationship to God is described by the word *peace* (Romans 5:1). The love of God is poured out within our hearts (Romans 5:5). How then do we deal with the anger that comes from our loss?

Again, I have no easy answers to give. I am not going to say anything *new*. The only answer I have is that God loves us, God has saved us, and God is good. Those are simple statements, but taken together, they tell us that we really have no basis for our anger. Instead, we must be willing to trust our loving Lord to do what is right.

Last year I lost a dear friend and mentor. Dr. D.C. Martin was a godly man who impacted many a student at Grand Canyon University in Phoenix, Arizona. I had the privilege of knowing him as a student and, briefly, as a colleague when I began to teach at Grand Canyon. I remember so many of his "Martinianisms," as we called them, but one that has really stuck with me had to do with the child's prayer "God is great. God is good. Let us thank Him for our food." Dr. Martin would often comment, "That prayer is tremendously profound. Take time to think sometime about what it means, and you'll be a better Christian for it." Dr. Martin was right. God is great. He is greater than you and I, and His purposes are far beyond our ability to even grasp, let alone judge. Yet God is good. We may at times be at a loss as to how a particular action of His is going to result in good, but God is good nonetheless. His goodness is not dependent upon my ability to see everything and understand everything. He is simply good. Because of that, He is to be thanked: for our food, for our lives, for our loved ones, and for the comfort He gives us in times of trial and distress.

Job and Mary

At the beginning of this book I spoke about my friend Mike and his little granddaughter, Autumn

Dawn. Just yesterday Mike and I were talking about how things are going. His reply took me back at first. "I feel like a cross between Job and Mary," he said. Noting the quizzical look on my face, he continued. "I feel like Job because I see Job sitting in his pile of ashes and his friends are trying to comfort him. They aren't doing a very good job, and God eventually comes along and says, 'Hey, I'm God, you are not. Get up and get back to your life. I have a purpose for you.'" I understood that part, but I then asked how Mary fit in. "Well," Mike replied, "I see Mary standing at the cross. She didn't leave. She didn't run away from that gruesome scene. She stayed there. So many are telling me to basically sweep away the picture of my little granddaughter lying dead in that hospital room, but I can't do that. I have to deal with the reality that she is really gone."

Job and Mary. Two different pictures of the complex process that is grief in the Christian life. Two biblical stories that speak to our human condition and, in their own way, give us hope. God comes to Job in the whirlwind and reminds Job of his creatureliness and inability to judge God. He picks Job up out of the ashes and sets him on his feet again. Job learns to trust in God even when he can't see the purposes in it all. And Mary. She stays with her Son even in His agony. She doesn't run away. She is honest with reality. She loves deeply and grieves just as deeply.

The Jewel of Bereavement

Charles Haddon Spurgeon once uttered these words:

> Tacitus tells us that an amber ring was thought to be of no value among the Romans till the emperor took to wearing one, and then immediately an amber ring was held in high esteem. Bereavements might be looked on as very sad things, but when we recollect that Jesus wept over his friend Lazarus, they are choice jewels and special favors from God. Christ wore this ring. Then I must not blush to wear it.

Have you been called, believer in Christ, to wear the golden ring of suffering, as did your Lord? Have you looked upon it as part of His gift of grace, or only as a painful ordeal of darkness? It makes all the difference in the world how you look upon it. Do you look upon your situation with earthly eyes that see only today, or do you look with heavenly eyes that see the landscape of eternity? You have been seated in heavenly places in Christ Jesus (Ephesians 2:6). Do you seek to have that vantage point in looking at your life and your grief? Paul said that we have been granted two gifts from God: to believe in Christ, and to suffer for Him (Philippians 1:29). Do you see these as gifts? If you do, you will have the key to grief: hope. If you are struggling with this, pause even now to ask God's grace to view your life, in its entirety, in the way He would have you to see it.

seven

Getting Through

A Brief Guide to Surviving the Grieving Process

Let's outline and review some of the major things to remember about the grieving process:

- Grief is natural. Everyone old enough to love is old enough to grieve.
- Grief takes time. The amount of time differs for each individual and is dependent upon the relationship that has been lost.
- Grief is individual. You can't compare your experience and your feelings to anyone else's. You are unique.
- Yet grief follows a pattern, and since we are all human beings, certain elements of the grieving process will be common.
- Grief is not always understood by others. Our society is poorly equipped to deal with death and grief.
- Grief makes us emotionally vulnerable. We are easily offended, hurt, and irritated.
- Grief deceives us in many ways. It tells us to remain isolated when in fact we need the companionship of others. It also deceives us into thinking

that we will only be well when we get "back" to where we were "before."

Remember as well some of the suggestions that have been made about how to handle grief:

- Don't expect the process to be easy or impossible; avoid both extremes.
- Don't compare the time it takes you with the time it has taken someone else.
- Draw on your preexisting support structures, that being your family, friends, and family of faith in church.
- Deal with issues, don't avoid them. Despite the temptation to give up or at least procrastinate, move ahead with necessary actions.
- Deal with belongings: avoid extremes. Don't just give everything away, keep what is special. But don't create "shrines."
- Expect unusual emotions. You may experience confusion more than ever before. Often people speak of feeling a weight upon their shoulders or their chest, holding them back.
- When you feel a good cry coming on, make it a positive experience by reflecting upon good memories.
- Think through and plan for holidays, birthdays, anniversaries, etc.

Reaffirming Life

As we come to the close of our brief discussion of grief and its role in our life, I want to encourage you as a believer in Christ to take advantage of the vast store of grace that is available to you in your Savior. In His wisdom He has given us the church, in which we find so many who can help us with our sorrows. I know in my own church my elders are men of such great wisdom and insight. Their lives are testimonies to God's grace. Hopefully you, too, have such men in your congregation. Seek their counsel and wisdom. God has given us one another for just such purposes.

If any one thing has helped people to refocus their lives and move back into a full and joy-filled life, it has been this: service to others. I have often counseled individuals who were stuck on the downward spiral of grief to volunteer their time to help others. In so doing I was helping them get out of their isolation while at the same time helping them to stop looking downward and inward. By helping others we find ourselves rejuvenated and reaffirmed. We see how we can be of help to others, and we become channels of God's grace. By serving others we help ourselves to experience the fullness of joy and living that God intends for us.

First and foremost we are servants of Christ. You remain His servant, even in light of the loss of your loved one. Do you think He still loves you? He does. He still asks for your service, even knowing you are hurting. He has a loving purpose, my friend. As you serve Him, He lives His life in you. He heals your heart, restores your soul. As you serve Him your life is enriched. And through it all, even if you can't see it right now, He is creating a beautiful image, a new creation, another portrait of Jesus Christ.

My father once told the story of how a goldsmith would purify gold. The goldsmith begins by placing the gold in the crucible and turning up the fire. As the gold melts, different impurities, being lighter than the heavy gold, float to the surface. The goldsmith carefully skims off the impurities as they come to the surface.

So it is with us. God is about doing something in our lives. He is making us like Christ. But we have many impurities that He is removing from us. Trials and difficulties are the fire that brings these things to the surface.

But what does the goldsmith do after removing the first impurities that appear? Does he stop? No, he makes the fire even hotter, bringing up the next level of impurities. The process continues on, each time requiring more and more heat.

And so it is with us. The purer we wish to be in His sight, the hotter the fire must be. Do we pray, "God, turn up the heat"? Or do we pray only for a break, a season of ease? If our hearts truly desire to be like Christ, we pray that He will continue His work of conforming us to His image.

Finally, do you know how the goldsmith knows when he has a pure product? How does he know he has finished his task? Quite simply, he knows he has accomplished his goal *when he sees his own reflection in the gold.* The impurities are gone, and nothing stands in the way of the gold reflecting his face.

Do you see what God is up to in your life? Can God see His reflection in your life, my friend? I know I want Him to be able to do that in my life, but I also know that He has a lot of purifying yet to do. The trials and difficulties I face—even the process of grief that we must endure when we lose a loved one—is part of how God makes us like Christ. When you see your grief as a means by which God is making you like Christ, you can begin to thank Him for His mercy and grace toward you. In hope you can say, "But as for me, I will watch expectantly for the LORD; I will wait for the God of my salvation. My God will hear me" (Micah 7:7).

BHP BOOKS BY JAMES R. WHITE

The Forgotten Trinity
The God Who Justifies
Grieving: Our Path Back to Peace
Is the Mormon My Brother?
The King James Only Controversy
Letters to a Mormon Elder
Mary—Another Redeemer?
The Roman Catholic Controversy
*What's With the Dudes at the Door?**
*What's With the Mutant in the Microscope?**

*with Kevin Johnson

Do you have comments?
Please address them to:

Alpha and Omega Ministries
P.O. Box 37106
Phoenix, AZ 85069

(602) 973–0318 (fax and message)

For faster response, contact us via E-mail:
orthopodeo@aomin.org

Visit our web page at
http://www.aomin.org
for information about Mormonism,
Jehovah's Witnesses, Roman Catholicism,
and General Apologetics, and
listings of debates, tapes, tracts, etc.